MEET ARIAN FOSTER

Football's Ultimate Rusher

Ethan Edwards

PowerKiDS
press
New York

Published in 2014 by The Rosen Publishing Group, Inc.
29 East 21st Street, New York, NY 10010

First Edition

Editor: Jennifer Way and Joshua Shadowens
Book Design: Greg Tucker
Book Layout: Andrew Povolny
Photo Research: Katie Stryker

Photo Credits: Cover, pp. 8, 18, 23 MCT/McClatchy-Tribune/Getty Images; pp. 4, 9, 13 Joe Robbins/Getty Images Sport/Getty Images; p. 7 Simon Bruty/Sports Illustrated/Getty Images; p. 10 J. Meric/Getty Images Sport/Getty Images; p. 12 The State/McClatchy-Tribune/Getty Images; pp. 15, 17 Ronald C. Modra/Sports Imagery/Getty Images; p. 16 Bob Levey/Getty Images Sport/Getty Images; p. 20 Grant Halverson/Getty Images Sport/Getty Images; p. 21 Marc Serota/Getty Images Sport/Getty Images; p. 24 John Biever/Sports Illustrated/Getty Images; p. 25 Boston Globe/Getty Images; p. 26 Christopher Polk/Getty Images Entertainment/Getty Images; p. 28 Jim McIsaac/Getty Images Sport/Getty Images.

Library of Congress Cataloging-in-Publication Data

Edwards, Ethan.
 Meet Arian Foster : football's ultimate rusher / by Ethan Edwards. — First edition.
    pages cm. — (All-star players)
 Includes index.
 ISBN 978-1-4777-2916-8 (library) — ISBN 978-1-4777-3005-8 (pbk.) —
 ISBN 978-1-4777-3076-8 (6-pack)
 1. Foster, Arian, 1984– 2. Football players—United States—Biography—Juvenile literature. I. Title.
 GV939.F68E38 2014
 796.332092—dc23

 [B]
                                    2013023114

Manufactured in the United States of America

CPSIA Compliance Information: Batch #W14PK2: For Further Information contact Rosen Publishing, New York, New York at 1-800-237-9932

Contents

One of the reasons Arian Foster is a great running back is that he is too big and strong to bring down with an arm tackle.

Arian Foster is one of the best **running backs** in the National Football League, or NFL. A running back's job is to run with the football. Sometimes it is handed to him. Other times he catches short passes. A running back must have great **agility** in order to avoid players on the other team's **defense**. Foster has great agility, speed, and power. In his spare time, he writes poetry. There are simply no NFL players like Foster. In fact, the Sporting News website called him "the most interesting man in the NFL."

All-Star Facts

Arian Foster is of African American and Mexican American descent. His first name is a shortened form of Aquarian, which means "water bearer" or "holder of knowledge," according to his father.

Arian Foster was born on August 26, 1984, in Albuquerque, New Mexico. His father was a former football star at the University of New Mexico. That is where he met Arian's mother. Arian grew up with a brother named Abdul and a sister named Christina. When he was seven years old, Arian's teacher asked the class what they wanted to be when they grew up. Arian decided he wanted to make it in the NFL. One day he would make that dream come true, even if the rest of the football world had counted him out.

In high school, the San Diego Union Tribune named Arian Foster the All-San Diego Western League Player of the Year.

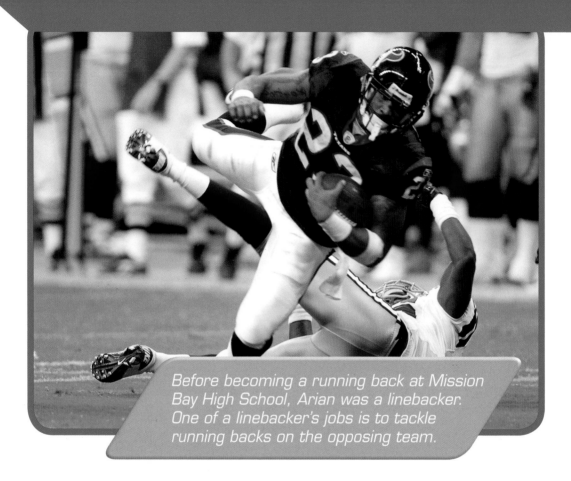

Before becoming a running back at Mission Bay High School, Arian was a linebacker. One of a linebacker's jobs is to tackle running backs on the opposing team.

Arian went to Valley High School and tried out for the football team. Unfortunately, he was not big enough to make the team. When his parents divorced, Arian went to live with his father in San Diego, California. He attended Mission Bay High School and tried out again. This time his father trained him, and this time he made the team.

In Arian's junior year, he had a great game in the **postseason**, during which he ran for 200 yards even though his team lost. He became the team's full-time running back in his senior year and collected more than 2,500 yards for the season. This was good enough for some top college **scouts** to take an interest in him.

In his senior year, Arian led San Diego County in all-purpose yards with 2,500. He scored 24 touchdowns in addition to six scores on kickoff returns.

Foster started attending college in 2004 at the University of Tennessee in order to play for the Tennessee Volunteers. Foster got the chance to prove himself during his freshman, or first, year when the starting running back was **injured**. Foster ran for 879 yards that season and had a brilliant game against Vanderbilt, during which he ran for 223 yards and scored two **touchdowns**. His 268 total yards from **scrimmage** were the third most in school history.

Here Foster tries to gain some yards against the Wisconsin Badgers, but he is tackled quickly.

Foster had a reputation for fumbling in big games, but he lost the ball only five times in four seasons and had a team-record 650 carries.

After a tough sophomore, or second, season, Foster bounced back with an excellent junior year. He ran for 1,193 yards and scored 12 touchdowns. NFL scouts began to watch him, hoping he would be a good pick for the NFL draft. Foster's coach talked him into staying for another season.

Unfortunately, Foster's senior year was not very good. He ran for only 570 yards and had two big **fumbles** that hurt his team. Coaches and players began to say that he did not get along well with teammates. These stories eventually reached the coaches and offices of NFL teams. Foster probably would have been picked early had he entered the draft after his junior year. The decision to return for his senior year put his NFL future on the line.

Foster was out for the majority of his sophomore season because of injuries. He ended the season with just 322 rushing yards.

Every year the NFL holds a **draft**. It is a system in which each team takes turns picking the best players. Every year, there are hundreds of players who are not chosen. It is very difficult for these undrafted players to make careers in the NFL. It is even rarer for them to become stars. At the end of the 2009 NFL Draft, Foster was among those undrafted players. His uneven college career hurt his chances. Teams wanted players they knew they could depend on, and he had a history of big fumbles in big games.

When Foster first started with the Houston Texans, he wore number 37. He now wears number 23.

Here Foster rushes against the Dallas Cowboys in a game during the 2010 season at Reliant Stadium. Reliant Stadium is the home stadium of the Houston Texans.

Foster did not give up. His girlfriend Romina researched NFL teams that might need Foster's skills. She thought the Houston Texans were worth a shot. The Texans signed Foster to their practice team. This meant he could not play in games but would practice against players on the team.

The team soon realized how skilled he was and signed him to the Texans as a **free agent**. Foster finally played in an NFL game on November 23, 2009. However, he played for **special teams**. A few weeks later, he finally got his chance as a running back against the Miami Dolphins. Foster scored a touchdown. He started in the next game against the New England Patriots and ran for 119 yards with two touchdowns.

According to Sports Illustrated, Foster ranked twenty-fourth among running backs available in the 2009 NFL Draft. He was expected to be chosen, but he went undrafted.

Record Breaker

Foster's patience paid off, and the Texans now believed in him. They could not believe their luck in signing such a talented undrafted player. Fans were eager to see what Foster could do in the 2010 season. He made history on opening day. In the very first game of the season, Foster broke a team record by rushing for 231 yards. He also scored three touchdowns. It was the best opening-day performance by a running back since O. J. Simpson ran 250 yards in 1973.

One of the reasons why Foster is an excellent running back is that he studies the playbook. He also studies the opposing teams' defensive plays.

Here Arian Foster outruns Michael Griffin for a touchdown during a game against the Tennessee Titans.

A few weeks later, Foster broke another team record with a 74-yard touchdown run. It was the longest run ever by a Texan. Foster finished the season by winning the NFL rushing title. That meant he ran for more yards than any other running back in the NFL that season. He also broke the record for most yards from scrimmage by an undrafted player.

Foster was selected to play in the Pro Bowl, which is a special game for which fans select the best players at each position. Foster suffered from injuries in the beginning of the 2011 season. He recovered and had some excellent games, especially against the Tennessee Titans. Foster collected 115 rushing yards and 119 receiving yards in a single game!

Arian Foster was chosen as the AFC Offensive Player of the Month in September 2010 and October 2011.

Many NFL experts agreed that Foster was the best running back in the game. However, the Texans had signed him as an undrafted free agent. That meant he was not being paid as though he were one of the best running backs in the game. Before the 2012 season, the Texans signed Foster to a new contract worth $43.5 million over five years. It often happens that players disappoint their fans after being signed for lots of money. There is suddenly a lot of pressure to live up to that paycheck. If Foster felt pressure, he did not show it. He had one of his best seasons yet in 2012.

Here Foster is congratulated after jumping into the crowd after a 42-yard touchdown run against the Cincinnati Bengals in a game that kept the Texans in the play-offs.

Foster holds many records with the Texans, including most rushing yards in a single season (1,616) and most rushing touchdowns in a single season (16).

On October 8, 2012 in a game against the New York Jets, Foster reached 5,000 career yards from scrimmage in what was only his fortieth game. Only two other players recorded 5,000 yards in fewer games. Foster was still making history.

He was also becoming famous. Fans across the nation became used to seeing Foster's touchdown celebration. Some players dance when they score touchdowns. Foster gives a *namaste* bow. He presses his hands together and bows. This is a show of respect and peace in India and other countries in Asia. Foster's *namaste* bow means that he respects the fans and the game of football.

The Houston Texans won 12 games and lost 4 games during the 2012 season. Their season ended when they lost to the New England Patriots in their second play-off game.

Foster attended the FedEx lemonade stand with Junior Achievement students in the Super Bowl XLVII Media Center. The event gave students the chance to run their first business.

Off the field, Foster likes to write poetry. He also listens to Mozart and reads Shakespeare. His poetry has helped him through difficult times, especially those times when no one believed in his football skills.

Healthy eating is important to Foster. He was a **vegan** for a time. This is a strict diet in which a person does not eat meat, milk, eggs, or any other animal products at all.

Foster and Romina married and have a daughter named Zeniah. Helping others is important to Foster. He helps charities like the Boys and Girls Clubs. He also works with A Crucial Catch. This is an NFL campaign that encourages people to be screened for cancer so that it can be detected and treated early.

All-Star Facts

Foster hosts a radio show on Sirius called the *Arian Foster Show*. He guest-starred as himself on an episode of the television show *Hawaii Five-0* that aired in 2013.

Against All Odds

Before the 2010 season, very few NFL fans had ever heard of Arian Foster. In a few short months, he became known as one of the top players in the NFL. It took only a few seasons for him to break some of the biggest records in the game. In those difficult early years, nobody believed in Foster but himself and his family. When he finally got the chance to prove himself, he was more than ready. Foster has a tattoo featuring the words "against all odds." The serves as a reminder that the experts are often wrong. The most important thing is to believe in oneself.

All-Star Facts

Arian Foster was the number-one pick in most fantasy football drafts in 2012. Fantasy football is a game in which users compete against each other as general managers of virtual teams.

On October 8, 2012, the Houston Texans beat the New York Jets, 23–17, at MetLife Stadium in East Rutherford, New Jersey.

Stat Sheet

Team: Houston Texans
Position: Running back
Number: 23
Born: August 24, 1986
Height: 6 feet 1 inch (1.85 m)
Weight: 228 pounds (103 kg)

Season	Team	Rushing Attempts	Rushing Yards	Rushing Touchdowns
2009	Texans	54	257	3
2010	Texans	327	1,616	16
2011	Texans	278	1,224	10
2012	Texans	351	1,424	15

Glossary

agility (uh-JIH-luh-tee) The property of being able to move around quickly and easily.

defense (DEE-fents) When a team tries to stop the other team from scoring.

draft (DRAFT) The selection of people for a special purpose.

free agent (FREE AY-jent) A player who is not signed with a team and who can sign with whichever team offers him the best contract.

fumbles (FUM-bulz) Dropping balls that the other team can pick up.

injured (IN-jurd) Harmed or hurt.

postseason (pohst-SEE-zun) Games played after the regular season.

running backs (RUN-ing BAKS) Football players whose job is to take or catch the ball and run with it.

scouts (SKOWTS) People who help sports teams find new, young players.

scrimmage (SKRIM-idg) The imaginary line between two football teams as they face each other to begin a new play. Also called the line of scrimmage.

special teams (SPEH-shul TEEMZ) The players who are on the field for kicking plays.

touchdown (TUTCH-downz) Getting the football behind the opposing team's goal line. A touchdown is worth six points.

vegan (VEE-gun) A person who follows a diet in which he or she eats no meat or other animal products.

Index

Websites

Due to the changing nature of Internet links, PowerKids Press has developed an online list of websites related to the subject of this book. This site is updated regularly. Please use this link to access the list: www.powerkidslinks.com/asp/foster/